SPORTS HEROES

AARON RODGERS

Sloan MacRae

PowerKiDS
press

New York

Published in 2012 by The Rosen Publishing Group, Inc.
29 East 21st Street, New York, NY 10010

First Edition

Editor: Jennifer Way
Book Design: Julio Gil

Photo Credits: Cover (main), p. 5 Jamie Squire/Getty Images; cover (background), pp. 7, 12, 22 Joe Robbins/Getty Images; p. 4 Kevin C. Cox/Getty Images; p. 6 Bill Frakes/Sports Illustrated/Getty Images; pp. 8–9, 11 (right) Steve Grayson/WireImage/Getty Images; pp. 10, 11 (left) Robert B. Stanton/WireImage/Getty Images; p. 13 Chris Trotman/Getty Images; p. 14 Doug Pensinger/Getty Images; p. 15 Scott Boehm/Getty Images; pp. 16–17 Robeck Beck/Sports Illustrated/Getty Images; p. 18 Jonathan Daniel/Getty Images; p. 19 Damian Strohmeyer/Sports Illustrated/Getty Images; pp. 20–21 Jason Merritt/Getty Images.

Library of Congress Cataloging-in-Publication Data

MacRae, Sloan.
 Aaron Rodgers / by Sloan MacRae. — 1st ed.
     p. cm. — (Sports heroes)
 Includes index.
 ISBN 978-1-4488-6161-3 (library binding) — ISBN 978-1-4488-6280-1 (pbk.) —
 ISBN 978-1-4488-6281-8 (6-pack)
 1. Rodgers, Aaron, 1983– —Juvenile literature. 2. Football players—United States—Biography–Juvenile literature. 3. Quarterbacks (Football)—United States—Biography—Juvenile literature. I. Title.
 GV939.R6235M33 2012
 796.332092—dc23
 [B]
                              2011022330

Manufactured in the United States of America

CPSIA Compliance Information: Batch #WW11PK: For Further Information contact Rosen Publishing, New York, New York at 1-800-237-9932

CONTENTS

⭐ NOT ALWAYS EASY

Aaron Rodgers is one of the most famous **quarterbacks** in America today. Getting there was not an easy journey. Rodgers plays for the Green Bay Packers in the National Football League, or NFL. The Packers have one of the richest histories in all of **professional** sports. No other team in the NFL has won as many **championships.**

As the Packers' quarterback, Aaron Rodgers calls the plays for the offense when they are on the field. »»

Many fans were surprised at Rodgers's success. There were times when the football **experts** counted him out as a player who could make it big in the NFL. Rodgers did not listen to them. In his heart he knew he was good enough. He proved them wrong on the football field.

Here is Rodgers (center) doing his famous championship belt dance. In the dance he pretends to put on a belt. He does this dance after the Packers make a great play.

5

TOO SMALL FOR FOOTBALL?

Aaron was born in Chico, California, on December 2, 1983. Aaron's father played football in college, so football was important to the Rodgers family. Aaron learned all about the game and started playing at a young age.

In high school, Aaron was a star quarterback. He hoped to keep playing football at a college with a good football program. Although he was a record-setting player, the colleges with the best football programs thought that, at 5 feet 10 inches (1.8 m)

Rodgers kept growing while he was in college. Today he stands 6 feet 2 inches (1.9 m) tall and weighs about 220 pounds (100 kg). This is a typical size for an NFL quarterback.

tall and 165 pounds (75 kg), Aaron was too small. They thought he could not play well against college players who were much taller and heavier. When he graduated, in 2002, Aaron did not have any college football **scholarship** offers.

Growing up, Aaron played football as well as Little League baseball. Rodgers focused on football in high school and worked hard to build muscle and be a better player.

★ A SMART PLAYER

Football takes brains, and quarterbacks need to be smart. A quarterback, such as Aaron Rodgers, leads his team's **offense**. A good quarterback also must be able to fool the other team's **defense** by guessing what they are going to do.

Rodgers helped lead Butte to a NorCal Conference championship. Here he is in 2003, after he transferred to the University of California, Berkeley, or Cal. >>>

Aaron proved himself to be a smart player. Since no big schools wanted him, he played football at a small college near his hometown called Butte Community College. In one year of playing for Butte, he led the team to a 10–1 record, or 10 wins and 1 loss. This earned Butte a conference championship. This great record got the attention of bigger college football programs.

FOOTBALL AT CAL

As a quarterback, Rodgers decides to whom to throw the ball for the best chance of scoring. Here he is playing quarterback for Cal in 2004.

The coaches at the University of California, Berkeley, liked what they saw in Aaron Rodgers's play as a quarterback. They could not believe that other **recruiters** had passed on him. They wanted Rodgers to transfer to their Division 1 school. It takes most junior college **athletes** two years to be allowed to transfer. Rodgers had excellent grades, though, so he was allowed to transfer after only one year.

Here you can see Rodgers in position as quarterback. By standing behind the offensive linemen, he can call and lead the team's plays.

Rodgers began his **sophomore** year at Cal in 2003. He led the Golden Bears to some of the biggest games in college football. After his junior year, Rodgers decided he was ready to leave college to try to join the NFL.

After Cal won the Insight Bowl game against Virginia Tech in 2003, Rodgers won the award for Most Outstanding Offensive Player. Here, he is holding the trophy for that award.

⭐ IN BRETT FAVRE'S SHADOW

Rodgers had high hopes that he would be picked early in the 2005 NFL **Draft**. Those hopes did not last long. The teams that needed new quarterbacks passed on picking Rodgers. Most head coaches did not think he was good enough or big enough to start in the NFL. Once again, the experts had underestimated Aaron Rodgers.

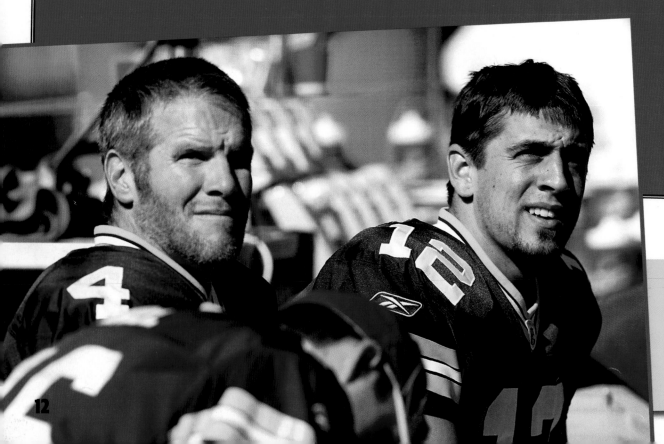

Here is Rodgers posing with a Green Bay Packers jersey shortly after he was drafted in 2005. He was later given the number 12.

The Green Bay Packers picked Rodgers. The Packers already had Brett Favre, one of the best quarterbacks ever to play the game. Rodgers had made it to the NFL, but it looked as though he would be used only as a backup for Brett Favre.

Brett Favre (left) was the Packers' starting quarterback for the first three seasons Rodgers was with the team. Favre had been with the Packers for many years and was a fan favorite, which meant Rodgers had a lot to live up to!

⭐ IN BRETT FAVRE'S SHOES

Rodgers played backup quarterback for his first season with the Packers. He thought he would be the starting quarterback in the 2006 season because many people thought that Favre was about to retire. Instead, Favre played for the Packers through the 2007 season and then moved to the New York Jets.

Here is Rodgers during a 2011 play-off game against the Chicago Bears. The Packers won this game, which meant the team would play in Super Bowl XLV.

Rodgers's chance to be a starting quarterback finally came in 2008. Many Green Bay fans did not think Rodgers was ready, though. They let him know that he had big shoes to fill. Rodgers was ready to fill those shoes. He threw for 4,000 yards in each of his first two seasons as a starter!

 Rodgers (center) is discussing a play with his Packers teammates during a 2011 game.

★ SUPER BOWL XLV

The most important game in the NFL season is the Super Bowl. This is the NFL championship game. Players dream of winning this game, but few even get a chance to play in it. Rodgers led the Packers to a great season in 2010, with a record of 10–6. This allowed the Packers to reach the **play-offs**.

Before Super Bowl XLV, the Green Bay Packers had not played in the Super Bowl since 1998. The Pittsburgh Steelers had last played in the Super Bowl in 2009 and had won that game. Rodgers (center) knew his team was in for a tough Super Bowl matchup!

The Packers won all their play-off games and earned a spot in the Super Bowl facing the Pittsburgh Steelers. It was a close game, played by two of the best teams in the NFL. In the end, the Packers won Super Bowl XLV, with a final score of 31–25.

⭐ MVP

The Steelers were not an easy **opponent** for the Packers to beat in Super Bowl XLV. The Packers had not played in a Super Bowl since 1998, but it was the Steelers' third trip to the Super Bowl in six years. The Steelers were one of the NFL's best teams. They had a great quarterback in Ben Roethlisberger and a very tough defense.

The Super Bowl trophy is called the Vince Lombardi trophy. Lombardi was the Packers' coach in the 1960s, when the team won the first two Super Bowls. Here is Rodgers holding the trophy after the Packers won Super Bowl XLV.

Rodgers was ready to face the Steelers. He played one of his best games ever. He even won the Most Valuable Player, or MVP, award. This means that he was the best player in that game. Green Bay fans were glad that Rodgers was their quarterback!

Here is Rodgers signing a Packers fan's coat before a home game at Lambeau Field, in Green Bay, Wisconsin.

★ OFF THE FIELD

Some stars find it difficult to deal with fame. Suddenly everybody loves them, and they have lots of money. This might not sound like a problem, but stars often struggle with the attention and expectations that fame brings.

Aaron Rodgers learned how to deal with success. He became friends with former quarterbacks such as Trent Dilfer, Troy Aikman, Kurt Warner, and Steve Young. These stars are **mentors** to Rodgers, and they give him advice about life on and off the field. Rodgers likes to give back to his communities, and he works with several **charities** in both Green Bay and his hometown of Chico.

Off the field, Rodgers sometimes attends charity events. Here he is at an event for a charity that helps poor women around the world start small businesses. ⟫

CIRCA
WORTH MOR

Eau de Nous
eaudenous.com

Mercedes-Benz

SEVEN BAR
FOUNDATION

Benz

ERTO RICO
ES IT BETTER

RICO
TER

es-Benz

FUN FACTS

 Aaron practiced throwing a football from a very young age. When he was only five years old, he could throw a football through a tire swinging on a rope.

 Growing up, Aaron's hero was the great quarterback Joe Montana of the San Francisco 49ers.

Aaron was a great basketball and baseball player in high school. He could throw a fastball 90 miles per hour (145 km/h).

Rodgers has visited American troops stationed in Alaska. He joined them in a bobsled race.

Rodgers owns a record label that produces rock music. It is called Suspended Sunshine Records.

 Rodgers's favorite movie is *The Princess Bride*.

 Rodgers does a funny dance every time he throws a touchdown. In the dance, he pretends to be a wrestler or a boxer putting on a championship belt.

 Rodgers is the first quarterback from the University of California to win a Super Bowl.

 Rodgers wears number 12. Many other great quarterbacks have worn this number, including Terry Bradshaw, Tom Brady, Joe Namath, and many others.

 Rodgers is the first NFL quarterback to throw for 4,000 yards in his first two seasons as a starter.

⭐ GLOSSARY

athletes (ATH-leets) People who take part in sports.

championships (CHAM-pee-un-ships) Contests held to determine the best, or the winner.

charities (CHER-uh-teez) Groups that give help to the needy.

defense (DEE-fents) When a team tries to stop the other team from scoring.

draft (DRAFT) The picking of people for a special purpose.

experts (EK-sperts) People who know a lot about a subject.

mentors (MEN-torz) Trusted guides or teachers.

offense (O-fents) When a team tries to score points in a game.

opponent (uh-POH-nent) A person or a group that is against another.

play-offs (PLAY-ofs) Games played after the regular season ends to see who will play in the championship game.

professional (pruh-FESH-nul) Having players who are paid.

quarterbacks (KWAHR-ter-baks) Football players who direct the team's plays.

recruiters (rih-KROOT-erz) People who look for new members of a group or team.

scholarship (SKAH-lur-ship) Money given to someone to pay for school.

sophomore (SOF-mor) A student in his or her second year of high school or college.

INDEX

WEB SITES

Due to the changing nature of Internet links, PowerKids Press has developed an online list of Web sites related to the subject of this book. This site is updated regularly. Please use this link to access the list:
www.powerkidslinks.com/hero/rodgers/